MW01087340

TO WILDNESS

TO WITNESS

TO WILDNESS

JULIA THACKER

WAYWISER

First published in 2025 by

THE WAYWISER PRESS

Christmas Cottage, Church Enstone, Chipping Norton, Oxfordshire, OX7 4NN, UK
https://waywiser-press.com

Editor-in-Chief
Philip Hoy

Associate Editors
Katherine Hollander | Eric McHenry | Dora Malech | V. Penelope Pelizzon
Clive Watkins | Greg Williamson

Copyright © Julia Thacker, 2025

The right of Julia Thacker to be identified as the author of this work
has been asserted by her in accordance with the
Copyright, Designs and Patents Act of 1988.

All rights reserved. No part of this publication may be reproduced, stored in a
retrieval system, or transmitted in any form or by any means, electronic, mechanical,
photocopying, recording, or otherwise, without the prior permission of both the
copyright owner and the above publisher of this book.

9 7 5 3 1 2 4 6 8

A CIP catalogue record for this book is available from the British Library

Paperback ISBN 978-1-911379-16-4

MIX
Paper | Supporting
responsible forestry
FSC
www.fsc.org FSC® C013056

Contents

Contents

III

IV

Contents

Foreword by Paul Muldoon

It was in 1960 that Robert Lowell, the preeminent American poet at a time when the notion of "pre-eminence" was still thought viable, so memorably held forth on the notion of contemporary poetry being either "cooked" or "raw."

Lowell's contention was that "cooked" poetry, the sort that might then have been produced by the likes of Allen Tate, John Crowe Ransom, Robert Penn Warren, Louis Simpson or Donald Hall, was "marvelously expert," though it often seemed "laboriously concocted to be tasted and digested by a graduate seminar."

When it came to the "raw," this was a poetry characterized by "huge blood-dripping gobbets of unseasoned experience," and was mostly "dished up for midnight listeners." Lowell was clearly thinking of the Beats, particularly Allen Ginsberg, whose *Howl and Other Poems* had appeared in 1956.

There was, Lowell concluded, "a poetry that can only be studied, and a poetry that can only be declaimed, a poetry of pedantry, and a poetry of scandal."

The occasion of Lowell's remarks on the state of American poetry was telling, given that they were included in his acceptance speech for the National Book Award. The book being honored was *Life Studies*, his game-changing collection of 1959.

Life Studies is a collection divided into four sections, each with its own method. The first section, "Beyond the Alps," explores Lowell's family history and his relationship with his parents. The second, "91 Revere Street," is written in prose and offers a series of autobiographical sketches that detail Lowell's childhood and early adulthood. The third section consists of odes to four writers. The final section, "Life Studies," includes such poems as "Skunk Hour" and "Waking in the Blue."

Almost seventy years later, *Life Studies* remains the single most influential book of poems of English language poetry of the second half of the 20th century and, now, the first quarter of the 21st. What's striking about this fact is that so familiar are we with first person "lived experience" narratives, including those driven almost entirely by "identity poetics," that we may easily overlook their main source.

I give this long preamble to the work of Julia Thacker because it is vital to its contextualization. Lowell's eccentric family members may be Boston

Brahmins of Beacon Hill but they are cut from the same cloth as Thacker's supermarket bag boys, sundry Good Ol' Boys, Jell-O connoiseurs, Georgian moonshiners, not to speak of regular attenders of tent revival meetings. Thacker writes movingly of a brother:

> As kids, we sprawled on starburst
> linoleum, glued to Star Trek, my brother
> so small he fit in the V of my legs.
> Battling neon-colored brains in a jar,
> we, navigators on the deck of a starship,
> controlled everything and so calmed
> the tempers of our house, the wind
> of slammed doors. What did my brother think
> when I ran away? That I got beamed up?

It may be instructive to set poems by Lowell and Thacker beside each other. Here's Lowell "Waking in the Blue":

> I grin at Stanley, now sunk in his sixties,
> once a Harvard all-American fullback,
> (if such were possible!)
> still hoarding the build of a boy in his twenties,
> as he soaks, a ramrod
> with a muscle of a seal
> in his long tub,
> vaguely urinous from the Victorian plumbing.

And here's Thacker in "Archaeology":

> Once I left a man while he was
> taking a bath. The door slammed
> and he leapt out of the tub, a tidal
> wave on the shag rug, slick
> and shining. I don't recall
> what the drama was about,
> only the tub, kidney-shaped,

> porcelain painted pink, its gold claws,
> its filthy rings of sweat, rose oil,
> hashish, sloughed off skin.

One might be forgiven for thinking that the man "taking a bath" is Stanley himself, while the uncle in Thacker's "God Awful" who "is forbidden to lift more than fifteen pounds" is a version of Lowell's "Uncle Devereux," with whom he spends a "last afternoon" and who was "dying of the incurable Hodgkin's disease."

In the case of Thacker, this is an America that is, even now, too rarely represented:

> My kin are falling out of beds and bathtubs
> as from a great height.
> For the family reunion, they dine at Applebee's,
> tethered to oxygen tanks. Study
> Technicolor menus like the Great Books.

In addition to mirroring the four-part structure of *Life Studies*, Thacker includes something of its range. There are prose poems such as "Author's Note" and "Grass Soup," with its litany "of fits and fevers" and "seven children abed," that bring back the prose memoir "91, Revere Street." There are more conventionally formal poems like "Braid Him Into The Earth" that, even in its title, conjures up Uncle Devereux and the speaker who blends the "piles of earth and lime,/ a black pile and a white pile."

One of the reasons why Lowell was so exercised by the notions of the "cooked" and the "raw" in his National Book Award acceptance speech was his own realization that *Life Studies* itself represents a shift from his own earlier formal style to his much more unbuttoned later style. To some readers, the collection may even represent a synthesis of those "two piles." This would explain Lowell's final musing on "When I finished Life Studies, I was left hanging on a question mark. I am still hanging there. I don't know whether it is a death-rope or a life-line."

For Lowell himself, and for writers like Julia Thacker, this combination of cooked and raw has indeed become no less a "life-line" than the oxygen tanks to which her extended family are so memorably tethered.

I want to sleep the sleep of apples,
far away from the uproar of cemeteries.

—Federico Garcia Lorca

I

Artisanal Moonshine

I alone refused to be baptized.
My cousins thought I was going to hell
but I only moved to Massachusetts
where snows are Biblical
and thinking is the local prayer.

I live with a man who can't sleep.
He reads the French Surrealists
aloud until sunrise, his voice
a field stubbled with hoarfrost.

Frost: a silver word,
pewter of Pilgrims. Thirty years
of evenings in the Plough and Stars
call for another round of spirits, fig-infused.

One swig and I'm wrapped in blackberry
bramble, the singing and stomping
clip-clop rhythm of loose floor boards.

At revival meeting, Uncle Odell stood
to testify he'd gotten a bad batch of hooch,
had visions, wrecked his Studebaker.
Still he crawled out unmarked.

Preacher baptized him the next Sunday
during an early cold snap.
Deacons waded into the shallows
to clear the ice floes.
They brought their mallets down
and broke the river's bones.

A last swallow and my name dissolves in silt.
When the bartender brings the check,
I'm apt to sign *Verda*, aunt of the lazy eye.

I have my mother's fear of water
and the maps of our palms have gone unread.
I'm all mixed up
like that.

Curriculum Vitae

I hymn. I chigger. I gristle. I curate boxes of glass doorknobs. Scrape loose tobacco from the seams of Ethel's pocketbook. I My Sin. I Shalimar. I gold clasp. I assemblage. I mess with the past. I do not lacrosse. Do not ledger. Do not collect rents. I ghost the tails of my father's shirts. Catalogue iron-shaped scorch marks. Heels worn to stubs. Chalk-colored shoe polish. Propeller planes. Lavender tonic for Nervous. I violet river ink blots on post cards. Lick envelopes so my tongue is glued to the roof of my mouth. I pony express. I do not swim. I do not ride. Except for human animals. I zydeco. I crackerjack. I have a weakness for the silver emulsion of mirrors. I oxidize. I rhapsodize. I carnival. And all the fortunes I tell are cloudy with chance of bruise. None of these ventures are big money makers. I red 78 acetate. I rent party. I cornbread crumble in buttermilk. My kin picnic in cemeteries so no one gets left out. Aunt Belle never married. She prefers the cracked bell laughter of strangers. Ring of ash trees. Now I can't stop thinking about cat's eye marbles lodged in the river bottom. Mayonnaise jar of elderberry tea bleached blonde by the sun. Hot spit of bacon grease. White dots on my mother's wrist.

Plum Jam

To be elbow-deep in a barrel,
arms gloved crimson,
to make of simple labor
prayer, to stop checking my
sheet-creased face in the rearview.
I no longer say *mirror*
although they populate the world.
Boulevards of shop windows.
Sweet bodies of water.
We don't speak about
the country of the old,
strolling unnoticed, dissolving
into sidewalks and salted air,
the practice of becoming
pure spirit, like vespers
sounding over the far north.
Today we must work
with our hands until they are
no longer hands, bells pealing,
my tongue red with plums.

Dear Earth

It has been snowing here for days. The roads have been salted. There has been an electrical storm in my father's mind with shortages and outages. His thoughts are blank as a deserted barn. His legs will no longer support his weight, but his heart, that aubergine thing, with its winded pipes, its whistles, its ventricles, its secret chambers, will not stop beating. We console ourselves at the winter farmers' market with scarlet turnips and a cider of fermented ginger.

Please excuse my father. He has an appointment to have his mouth stuffed with roses. His body will be shipped to Appalachia per his request. He will be traveling alone, the casket tagged. He is solitary. His preference is to journey by land along the rutted roads and steep mountain drop-offs. He wishes to be interred alongside his drunkard father. Earth, make a place for him. Lay him down among the young Unionists whose eyes are cold marbles in the old daguerreotypes. Let his bones mingle with shale, fragrant peat, veins of coal. Let them kiss the amber shards of moonshine bottles and sea-blue Mason jars. There will be no benediction.

Today we put on not one but two horsehair shirts buttoned to the neck. Here we abide and silence is a virtue. I live exceedingly far north of the Kentucky mountains. One day I will be ash and pearls of bone scattered along the rocky coast of New England, beside the Algonquins vanquished by a plague of measles, among the bleached ribs of sperm whales, of barristers and stuffy transcendentalists. I am married to a Quaker who comes home stamping his heavy boots, eyebrows salted with frost. We do not hate our parents. Once we did. Now our memories are like muslin curtains, bleached by the winter sun. My husband loves me. Each night I lie down with him in the trundle bed. He has become brotherly.

For my husband and I are elders among the wild tattooed children, tribal in their beards and flannel shirts. The lenses of my eyes are brittle. When I look out onto the world, it is impressionistic, blurry. I believe this a kind of radiance. Earth, I wonder about your temperament. You shift and moan in your sleep. Please admit my father. I want it to be over. I want it to end. I write on a tablet of snow and the season is changing. Blackberry ink runs, smudging the ice-glazed windows. I am sincerely yours.

Dead Letter Office

Late in my career, I appoint myself Post Mistress
of the Dead Letter Office. Mute bell
above the door. I sort and catalog wine-stained
aerograms addressed in foreign tongues,
indecipherable postcards, their pewter shadows.
Stuff my pockets with messages
smuggled from prison camps, pages
torn from ledgers, envelopes left
to the elements, cursive smudged to watercolor.
Twine-wrapped packages of 19th century pornography,
large-breasted women in striped stockings
corsets pulled to their waists, their nipples
like roses, legs splayed open on velvet settees.
Into the waistband of my worsted wool skirt
I tuck cipher sheets from the madhouse,
declarations from fallen soldiers.
I drink the blue elixir of their fountain pens.

A Guide for Caregivers

In the warehouse of antique fathers,
call things by their names:
salt, fork, mercy, butter.

To him, loner, hoarder
of aluminum TV dinner trays,
luster after telephone books
dating back to 1961,
collector of wheat pennies.

Answer questions simply but clearly.
    I am your daughter.
    I have no children.
    I am not acquainted with anyone named Goddamned Glorie.
    I live hundreds of miles away.
    You cannot leave with me.

Allow yourself to be introduced as
the aforementioned Glorie.
If you are addressed by the names
of the dead, rise and offer your hand.

When he says even the rich
will enter Heaven barefoot,
agree, for your old one is already
washed by strangers, his ass wiped,
naked as the moon.

Do not take the hand of the retired history teacher
with the snazzy button-down and honeyed voice.
Do not lead him to his room and straighten
family pictures on the walls or fold
the afghan on back of his recliner.
Do not think, *Who would know?*
It is too late to go shopping for fathers.

Do not say, Tomorrow.
Do not say, Dad, we are not in Belgium,
We're in Dayton, Ohio
on the Midwestern plain of industrial farms
where cattle are pumped full of drugs,
corralled, fattened, felled and shipped
by rail. We are in the great Midwest
and the downtowns are empty
as though there has been a great war.

Do not recite the names
of drugs on his chart: Zoloft,
Aricept, Depakote Sprinkles.
Do not say, Father, I am like you.
Do not mention the bottle
of Xanax in your carry-on.
Do not say, We will explode like stars.
The skies will open. Our sleeves
will be empty and full of wind.
Our cells like constellations replicating
every day with errors.

How to Make Dandelion Wine

Wait for the afternoon heat. Let the sun
open and dry many flowers. Tarry.
If you are in love with a married man,
wade into fields and back yards. Keep low
to the ground. Pick before the first seeds have flown.
Look for yellow of #2 pencils. Van Gogh's straw bundles.
Collect one gallon blossoms per gallon wine.
Snip off stems and discard each green
collar. Drop in boiling water.
Petals will rise to the top.
Let cool. Test on inside of forearm like baby's milk.
Add four cups sugar, cake yeast, zest
of lemons. Cover with clean T-shirt.
About two weeks. Long enough
to forget his hands, a balcony,
butter-colored towels.

3 Odes

To Grief

I buckle your seatbelt, drive you deep
into the woods, as we hum
radio tunes. Then static. For miles
we cruise the frost-dark
forest, our windows green squares.
Then I pull over,
unbuckle you. Put a sack over
your drowsy head, push, and yell *Run*.
You stumble in circles.

*

To Creative Nonfiction

My step-father raised his rifle
to eye-level. We had driven his old, sick cur
miles out of the city, the mutt shedding
matted fur all over the backseat.
He released her into the woods,
tossed rocks. The dog whimpered,
ran, then paused and
looked at him quizzically.
They had been together for ten years.
Another smatter of stones.

*

To Wildness

Just yesterday, 2 a.m.
a pawing at my door. I cracked it open.
I can't describe the thing
that made its way back to me,
sunburnt, tick-stuck, smelling
of sour piss, half-frozen. I knew
it was mine. How could I not
open my arms to it?

For an Abandoned Library in Detroit

Chancellors of the Sky, Provosts of Rain:
I wish to report saplings rooted
in cracked checkerboard tiles, upended,
thick with sod. And young maples—
one sprung up to the second floor, towed by sunlight—
brushing volumes shelved on the balcony.
A tangle of sumac and wild grape vines
have overrun the study carrels.
There is a hole in the ceiling.

Downstairs, a globe sits in its cradle.
Cathedral windows still intact.
I must note the card catalog collapsed
on its haunches, the encyclopedia splayed out
accordion-style. Inside rain-plastered pages
of *War and Peace,* the Russian Empire
has been bored by earthworms.

Small combustions erupt,
ignited by pulp writers who snigger
and smoke in the stacks. I wish to report
illuminated manuscripts swollen and sunburnt;
a libretto, wind-chapped; leather-bound books,
male and swarthy, sprouting mushrooms;
Middlemarch velveted pool-table green.

Chancellors, withhold your garland of winds,
your hurricanes with Christian names.
The clouds are darkening like ink
smudged on a printer's hands.
Squalls gust in their wake.
Allow this newly feral world to unravel
slowly. Let this repository stand.

For the sake of the minor scholar who napped
in Special Collections for two decades

dreaming of Lorca's olive trees.
For the Polish violinist harboring a paperback
copy of *Lolita* overdue since 1962.
For my Uncle John, thirty years on an assembly line
who one afternoon watched the new welder fall
from the catwalk into a ladle of hot steel.
My uncle who reported to his shift the next day
and afterward walked to the library
and stared into a book
as though it were a tablet of water.

Doxology

Buzzed on Kool-Aid and ginger snaps,
we build a temple from Popsicle sticks.
My friend Mona sees Jesus's face
in a piece of toast. O land of milk and honey,
false idols, Red Sea parting. Verses flow
at Vacation Bible School. We wear our silver
crayons down to nubs, angeling the afterlife.

Sixteen and without mercy, I declare myself
atheist. From kin unmoored.
Bereft of: Beatrice, Roxie, Pollye, Etta.
O leopard-spandex Jezebel.
No husband! No children! Heathen!
Rumors abound. Vintage sweaters, moth-eaten,
rhinestoned, pearled.

I am my own god, my own high priestess.
Mine own book of timothy. Tent revival,
mud and silt, river risen, my own baptism.
Protector of *sayeth*, *goeth*, *It came to pass*.
My own pharaoh, linen-spooled, lavender-
doused. Pickle my heart in cassia and cinnamon.
Gold my mask.

God Denies Any Knowledge of Dead Angel in His Bed

He searches Heaven's cabinets for a hangover cure.
Combs knotted stars from his beard.
Sets the morning agenda. To the blind shepherd
he dictates a note: *The wind is blue.*
And what of tsunamis, wars?
Macedonian wells infested with bees?
God has a headache. His hands tremble.
He cannot look at the heap of sheets,
her celestial body, marcelled bob, cold
in his chamber. No one understands
that he is full of *duende*. Not the swarm of angels,
their platinum regiment rapping
at his windows, rattling doors, voices sharp
and clear, *Why?* God covers his ears.

II notes toward an elegy

*(**She calls her second husband Unfortunate Mistake and the
third Bigger Mistake**)*

Once I resided, a curl the size of a pig's knuckle
below her pelvic bone. They sliced her
down the middle to extract me
then fastened her with surgical buttons.
Her C-section scar a purple welt. Navel herniated.
Teeth gone bad because babies
leech calcium. Dimples and dentures.
On the run from this husband or that,
she checks us into The Starlite Motel.
I drive our Corvair convertible.
Afternoons, we lounge poolside as cars swish by.
We blister. Our skin peels off in sheets.

(*She blotted lipstick on our report cards, the backs of light bills*)

A girl in the Cumberland Mountains, she ironed God's white shirts.
Forgot sheets on the line overnight, wind-knotted sails of frost.
Wed the football captain, Garland, 4F and bitter.
Stepped out of loose clothes.
Horsehair-sofa honeymoon, cold cream for lubricant.
She worked in a munitions factory beside German prisoners
of war, ordered not to look the blond boys in the eye.
V for Victory. All the silk for parachutes.
She concocted leg paint from tea. Drew seams
up the backs of her calves with eyebrow pencil.
Read fan magazines in the bath.
What hobbies do you share with Rita Hayworth?
    Candlepin bowling.

*(**Pretend you are in prison, glad for one cracker, one stalk of celery**)*

Will I prepare her body? Swipe her lips with Revlon
Cherries in the Snow, Persian Melon? She buys herself
greeting cards, Valentine's, St. Patrick's, Thanksgiving
and signs them *From your cold-hearted daughter.*
Bundles for me to find when I come home.
She becomes a fraternity housemother
and resides in a converted garage. At Spring Fling,
shows off her jitterbug. Teaches pledges the Rock Step,
the Cuddle.

(She was the height of a Renaissance suit of armor)

The first time a man gave her roses, she was 67.
He took her for cod cheeks in tarragon sauce.
When she died I found the menu in her Bible.

(*She kisses the Orchard Manor attendants, her minimum-wage daughters*)

She steps out of loose clothes
for weekly weigh in. Loss, loss, loss.
She claims the Home shows her bathing
on the evening news. All the glass
she breaks. A swan. A mirror.
Nude, she strolls to the common area.
Must they call the daughter?
At her post, a Queen Anne chair,
she awaits her subjects.

(She is falling, falling)

Out of bed, out of bathtubs, out of cypress trees.
She bequeaths her river-riven heart,
fake knee, honeycomb brain. At Christmas,
she looks like a starved horse, skin
hanging in folds. A row of girls
in white bonnets line the hall, a sprig
of violets in the snow.
I know they aren't real she says.

III

Julia

Latinate feminine form of Julius in use throughout Antiquity
(e.g. Saint of Corsica). Becoming rare during Middle Ages.
Revived only in the Italian Renaissance, **J** ornamented with foliage
and grotesques, strangled by vines. In dictionary bumping heads
with juju, jujube, juke. Forming part of *adieu*.
In my mother's voice, jewels. Five letters drowning. Aromatic.
During our Dark Ages, she christens me Phony, Harlot, Bad With Money.
Says not to address her as Mother. I may call her June
or Bitch. Our battlements, our distance, inflected in clipped declaratives.
Pass the salt. As though we had never shared a body.
For years, I will not take her hand
until she is old, a ruin, who can't remember my name.

Advice from the Afterlife

Do not take nightshade into your body.
Tomatillos, cayenne, chili peppers, berries of belladonna.
Remember your tendency to swell. Do not swallow
the summer dark. Do not get above your raising   *raining*.
I am still your mother.

God Awful

In the pine woods of North Georgia, my uncle
is forbidden to lift more than fifteen pounds.
What does that mean, he asks.
Bushel of sleigh bells? Newborn calf?

Aunt Roxie sleeps fenced
by a metal railing. She bums smokes,
sips whiskey from teacups, sloshes
spirits onto her nightgown.

When my father's doorbell chimes,
he picks up the telephone and holds it to his ear.
Says he hears the stars.

My kin are falling out of beds and bathtubs
as from a great height.
For the family reunion, they dine at Applebee's,
tethered to oxygen tanks. Study
Technicolor menus like the Great Books.
Swap rumors of a cousin's last words:
water, Gatlinburg, damnation.

Oh, I have questions.
Does the soul flit from jug
to hurricane lamp to pocketbook,
poor thing, looking for a container?

Now when I talk about my people,
I mean a growing army of ghosts.
When I say *us*, I mean myself,
heiress to Zoot suits, a German Luger.

Now when I dial, rotary phones ring
in the branches of wet ash trees.

Paperwork

Unfolded, the decree itself is onionskin,
like airmail filled in with your parents'
names: June and Russell, the looped *R*
smudged and missing its staff.
When you unearth the envelope
from your father's safe deposit box,
official blue and soft with age,
you think of that typewriter
as animal, its noisy pulse,
the clacking metal racket
of the Smith Corona,
the beauty of an antique font.
You think of the secretary typing
into late afternoon on her fourth cup
of coffee, Empress of Serifs
and Dissolution of Marriages,
fingers punching keys,
staring into the legal document
as if it were luster, the blue
envelope, a piece of sky.

Author's Note

Raised in the hollows, I write under the pen name Mae on the Morrow. I have worked as a ventriloquist for the dead. Also as an apothecary grinding seahorses to powder, prescribing lavender boughs for sleep. Thrice divorced, I tend wedding gowns like orchids under glass. Currently betrothed to vermillion, I reside in virgin forest outside Boston, feasting on strawberries, beets, radicchio. Publications include a memoir of my father. I left out the ringing in his ears, fresh cut grass in his trouser cuffs. I have a lazy eye. Among my honors is a fellowship from the Institute of Doused Lighthouses. I may be reached by passenger pigeon.

All the Flowers Are for Me

By the fistful, licorice-black, Georgia clay-red,
cheddar-yellow pills pressed into my palm.
Remedy for doughy arms, belly, thighs.
A doctor writes the scrip and I'm wide awake
for three consecutive sunrises, scribbling
in a spiral notebook indecipherable inky knots,
Even the teenage poems perspire through their clothes.
I eat only flavored lip gloss and lemon Jell-O.
Krishna swallowing forest fires, fields of marigolds.
Teetering on platform shoes, dazed,
doll-size, I spread my bramble of hair
across the ironing board, press one hank at a time,
iron hissing, singed. Smell faintly of smoke.

.

Black Hole

My brother is stoned, his pupils black marbles.
The day our mother dies, he smells like weed,
says, *If you had to nail up wallboard in rich peoples'*
houses all day, you'd fucking love dope too.
Late to the funeral, he sits in back of the church.
Steps out during the eulogy to toke up.

My brother plays bass in a band called Ebola.
A pit bull guards his days and nights, guards
his four sons from three drive-by mothers.
I've watched his boys rake a stash
delicately, pick out stems and seeds.
When the union schedules a drug test,
the youngest pees into a plastic cup
and ratholes it in my brother's jacket.
What I know about these children
I could bellow into a field.

As kids, we sprawled on starburst
linoleum, glued to *Star Trek*, my brother
so small he fit in the V of my legs.
Battling neon-colored brains in a jar,
we, navigators on the deck of a starship,
controlled everything and so calmed
the tempers of our house, the wind
of slammed doors. What did my brother think
when I ran away? That I got beamed up?
He must have searched my empty bed,
the galaxy of linoleum, all the places
I was not. The backyard. The sky.

Conjoined Twins Plead, "Put Us Back Together"
Brothers Unhappy Since They Were Separated 45 Years Ago

Her blue dress with yellow cornflowers
damp at the waist, she at the sink evenings.
Talcum powder caked in the creases of her neck
where we nest. The ungainly sail of our diaper
rigged by duck-shaped pins.
On muggy days she lays us on a divan,
spins nautical tales, window fan creaking
like the rig of a schooner.
She'd rather have been a sailor
than the wife of Old Pa.
Are we *ungodly*?
He says so. When company comes,
hides us behind a folding screen.

Only *she* makes us laugh,
displaying a potato with many eyes and tendrils.
Boils us bone-broth for strength.
Purees purple carrots for sight.
At bedtime, reads the *Encyclopedia Brittanica* aloud:
In ancient Rome, a pound of ginger
equals the price of a sheep.
But we do not know how to tie our shoes.
Our walking halted,
four legs, four arms waving.
Are we an insect on its back?

A strip of cartilage tethers us
at the sternum. Men of medicine
set upon us with instruments, unfasten us.
Ether-asleep, we call for Ma.
We wake apart.
Nights, we cry gales until she
places us side by side in the old crib.

Conjoined Twins Plead, "Put Us Back Together"
Brothers Unhappy Since They Were Separated 45 Years Ago

As in most tales, years pass.
Undertakers ferry our parents to Rest Haven.
We, widowed of them, wobble on sea legs
one-and-a-half leagues to the 7-Eleven
for donuts and milk. Jim, the proprietor,
says he has never seen men so pale.
We are like Old Pa
stationed in front of the black
and white TV, arms laced, foreheads twinned.

Bigfoot Walks Among Us

We ate ants peeled from bark, a rain of plums
when he rattled the trees. Lumbering. Shackled.
He stripped me and I flew up, a wood moth on birch
eyeing the girl below, her limbs spread five point star.
After, he offered jackrabbit on a spit, tinctures.
I covered myself with fir branches. Mostly I was alone.
I gave up counting the days, hair wilding on my legs, arm pits forested.
Gagged on my own sour smell. While he sloshed through creeks
and villages, I crawled along the thick moss floor, picked
snow-capped mushrooms, pigweed, prickly lettuce.
Tongue furry, teeth velveted, I learned to suck spearmint.
In snow, he hollowed a deer, laid me inside the carcass.
My dreams tasted of iron; antlers, a crown I wore lit with fire.
Sometimes he took me along miles of hemlock and sequoia.
Evenings, we crouched at wood's edge, spied the far lights.

Later I was offered a heart-shaped swimming pool for my story.
Did he make you do things?
My throat clogged with birdsong. My mind, with leaves.

How to Get Released from the Hospital

Dress fully in your shoes of paper.
Accept Dixie cups of pills
the color of Easter eggs. Orange juice.
Swallow. Stick out your tongue.
Join yoga in the Rec Room. Share.
Ignore attendant shadowing you
and taking notes. Journal. Sketch a door
of bottle glass. A long complicated sentence
with hairpin turns and arrows. Sanction
your husband's plan to hide all but
the butter knives. When the counselor
says, *You are the most functional patient
on the most functional unit*, do not ask,
But what am I in the world.

Please bring camphor compresses, a plate of sky, a glass of dusk.
To revive fried lilies dissolve aspirin in sugar water. Make me
a pillar of crystal, Lot's wife turning back to the city.
Because she will not give up worldly things, we call her Salt, Diamond
of the Dead Sea, but she does not answer. She sings in her sleep,
head ringing. As a child, I thought death meant *pause*
a few weeks of oblivion. I thought *pass away* meant
boarding a train at Grand Central. Dusk after dusk
face pressed to the window, past pale barns and bridges
collapsed in snow. To disembark nowhere
and wade in witchgrass to my knees. Here
is a field, whoosh of deep shaft mining. Here is an ocean
stretched along brackish pond flats
like a pearl necklace, rendered salt and mistaken for light.

Ode to Xanax

My white leash, my birch forest
felled, my exhausted frost-
encrusted bark, *Girl in a Coma*
buzzing on the radio, my albino
wreath and alabaster chachkas
white Jesus, wafer on the tongue
my mute button, my fog forecast
calla lilies, their throats, their chokehold
my dirty martini, White Russian
stash of ivory tusks, my whitewashed
history, will written in whetstone
my Arctic breath, lightheadedness
virgin powder visions and man made
snow, igloo, opium trance, windows
whited out, my avalanche.

In the Library at the End of the World

Knowledge is over.
Through hail storms and smashing
glass, I sleep too much.
Words drown, smudge and swell.
I fish a bulbous novel from the waters
and Anna Karenina flings herself.
It is snowing in St. Petersburg.
In Special Collections, booklice confetti
Thoreau's letters, blizzard Walden Pond.
Before the shuttering, a woman ripped a page
from an Illuminated Bible and ate it.
I have been here so long books remember
when they were trees. Burled. Crowning.
The Reading Room dense with forest.
We jigger sap from maples and boil it in great
vats, the rotunda redolent with burnt sugar.
Deferring to ash and alder, I, one of the ignorant
folk who roost in the branches.

"I Still Had Two Friends Left, But They Were Trees"

—Larry Levis

I still had teachers, but they were rivers.
One parched, choked with silt.
Her lessons, difficult and dark.
The other was a tributary
feeding great oceans like ink spilled
slowly across a continent.

Renaissance, recognizance, séance, mood-
lighting. I still had ex-lovers, should-have-
beens, synonyms for *regret*. The glass shells
of phone booths in which one might confess.
I still had a stew of tongue in apricots
and parsley. The first night alone in a movie
palladium. On the screen a park in fog.
Chalk lines around a body.

I still have my dead who wear their coats
inside out and drink from birdbaths.
Having forgotten language, they climb
cottonwood trees and whistle
in the high branches. In their honor
I wind clocks and shell peas.
Record their names in invisible ink.
In return, they stay until I fall asleep.

IV

Braid Him Into the Earth

Knee-high coffin of wicker, earth-boat floating through the woods.
Wrap him in heather, the old way. Hold a pocket mirror under his nose.
Say of him what we say of fathers.

If one of you has a three-string, then a tune.
Boots, stamp away spirits. If the ground is frozen,
dig shallow, spade ringing through ice, shale, mica-shine.

Lower the basket in a tangle of ginseng root, because I can't.
Let well water seep into crevices, mineral, like nickels
on the tongue. Skin freckling in feldspar, beetle, slug.

If flood waters drift the body loose, let him not be found by a child.
Let bones wash up with clay pipes, beads, thumb-size skulls.
Let them whiten and scatter in blond fields.

Grass Soup

Of Celts. Stew of pig knuckles and carrots. Of smelt iron. Of Orla. Lethe.
Maude. Growing old, growing onions. On Sunday boot black. Two wings
of rouge. Of weak bones, wind-chipped, pocked with holes. Dowager's
hump. Of eyes watery blue, pea green. Nearsightedness. Passable singing.
Sunless. Of fog. Of lusty gales. Skin the color of flour. Of chapped hands.
Viking crown dug up with the potatoes. Of rocky coast. Of peat burning.
Rendered fat. Potions, poultices. Hut thatched. Choked with smoke. Of
urine soaked. Of fits and fevers. Of blue babies. Of Limbo. Laid out in the
parlor. Nickels for eyes. Of whiskey-breath. Blackouts. Bottles jangling.
Of bobbin lace. Twins apace. Seven children abed. Of cabbage farts. Notes
stashed in straw. Of boiled laundry. Work shirts, their sour moons of sweat.
Of fiddles. Of trick knee and long prayers. Of haunt and pestle. Of thee.

Great-Great Grandfather Thacker Talks in My Ear

We are fed milk-soaked bread
from a bakery manned by convicts.

On my chin, the crumbs of a killer,
the falsely accused. What does it matter,

hands kneading flour, yeast, salt.
My hours numbered.

Our cots in military rows.
Bedpans clang and I call out

shyly, confused as to the century.
Is this my voice

or the river's. Laudanum-dosed,
I dream a stack of limbs

outside the tent, bonfire spitting
sparks into the cold.

By glow of oil lamps, nurses flutter
like a plague of moths

and I step out of this skin.
Brethren, I surrender.

Girl Buried with Finch

She gathers kindling in the forest. Day dreams.
Milk-white pallor. Sings. Soprano like glass.

Stuffs dandelions in her mouth.
Behind poplars, soldiers watch. Circle her.

One offers a honey stick to suck. Laughs
at her ardor. Her suckling. If they form a line,

present their cocks, mushroom-rank smell,
she can hold her breath and suck until

the jackdaw caws. After, they tie a bell
around her ankle with red string.

Die in a forest, buried in a forest. Farthest
cave. A chamber. Fill her mouth with the head

of a finch. Feathers. May her spirit be a bell.
A haunt. A bird for the next life.

Bag Boy Works Harder Now That He's a Ghost

Ribbed squash, king-pumpkin with its thick curling
stalk. Persimmons, verily orange and magenta, the weights
of sunsets in my hand. Egg-shaped plums shivering
on the conveyer belt. Cartons of milk perspiring,
wobbling toward me. Loaves of bread so light they bounce.
They want to float above us like balloons.
Bananas on stumps marked with bruises, the blind potatoes,
beets and rutabagas so rudely pulled from the earth, roots
still trailing a sprinkling of dirt.
The lemons are tropical, sunlight glowing
from within, while the beheaded cauliflower rolls
processional down the belt. Knock-kneed and sly,
a hairy kiwi masks its sweetness.
Vintage cheeses with red rinds, cellar-damp
like great-grandfathers who remember seamed stockings.
An amber bottle of port wears their fingerprints.
Let me touch them as they pass.
Let me sweep up the shadows
of my boot prints and store them in a locked box.

Last Will and Testament

I try on being forgotten,
lie with bees clustering in a lupine field
and Hereby Bequeath: a white splint,
ghosts sulking in the eaves, ears clogged with clover.
Napoleon decreed his head be shorn upon death
and from such hair bracelets made with tiny gold clasps.
Likewise, I leave a feral braid wrapped in cellophane.
Revoking all prior prayer and Codicils,
I gift a domicile on the flood plain. If the chimney is plugged,
fan smoke from the parlor. If holes
in the roof, squint at stars. I don't like the pallor of Heaven.
When asked about God, I say we're divorced.
I'm weary of my name on documents, its J and T,
loops and tall hat donning. Sky
is just a streak across the top of the paper.

Auto-Cento

In the warehouse of antique fathers
Persimmons verily orange and magenta

Loaves of bread so light they bounce
Float above us like balloons

Fathers baptized in lemon Jell-O, river risen, river-riven
Calla lilies, their pallor of Heaven

They kiss amber shards of moonshine bottles
Search loose floorboards for a hangover cure

Twine-wrapped packages of pornography, women in striped stockings
Nipples like roses, corsets pulled to their waists

Falling out of bed, out of bathtubs, out of cypress trees
All the silk for parachutes

In the warehouse, hold the sky like a bowl
Do not swallow the summer dark

Fathers, we must work with our hands
Until they are no longer hands

Winding clocks and shelling peas
Ironing God's white shirts, heap of sheets

In the warehouse of antique fathers, please excuse my father
He has an appointment to have his mouth stuffed with roses

Please excuse his violet river ink blots on post cards
Christmas wreath bleached blonde by the sun

His *goddamned*, his lusty gales, lightheadedness
His heart, that aubergine thing, its winded pipes, its whistles

Soul Wears a Crown of Milk Thistle

Sometimes she is buried at sea
wrapped in linen, the waves like mouths
of glass. Sometimes she rises again,

mollusk-pearled, and strolls the village
dripping kelp. No hymn, no pilgrimage, no
wafer on the tongue. She eschews hallelujah.

Refusenik of frankincense and myrrh.
Sometimes she claims she's just off the boat,
amnesiac. Takes the name Augusta Agnes.

Washes her unmentionables
at the sink. Bleaches her mustache.
Vagrant Sundays spent rolling in hay,

sun-warm, indistinguishable from dry grass.
No bathing costume, she swims in her drawers.
Wades in cranberry bogs. Eats tomatoes off the vine.

Sleeps on the beach. Sand makes a dune of her body.
At church bazaars, she filches Chesterfields
and barters for lace mantillas. Disappears for days.

Ignores my pleading letters penned in blackberry ink.
Neighbors say I should keep her on a leash.
She restoreth. She maketh still.

Archaeology

Once I left a man while he was
taking a bath. The door slammed
and he leapt out of the tub, a tidal
wave on the shag rug, slick
and shining. I don't recall
what the drama was about,
only the tub, kidney-shaped,
porcelain painted pink, its gold claws,
its filthy rings of sweat, rose oil,
hashish, sloughed off skin.
That fishing village is gentrified now.
Claw foot tub pulled out by the root,
half buried in a field, faucet clogged
with sandy loam, a Roman aqueduct,
bare-boned. *rim   lip   shoulder*
Vessel that cradled me —
I no longer recognize myself.
The way cod wrapped in brown
paper forgets the sea.

I Dreamed I Was Venus de Milo

A scatter of crows came to me
and I could not refuse them. Lighting
on my shoulders. Shit pearled on marble.
Sea-goddess Amphitrite. They spoke my true name.

Again in the seaside bungalow I wake
to the note you left *Playing Chess, X.*
Code for shooting up behind Spiritus.
Typing visions all night. At Blessing of the Fleet
you wrapped yourself in the flag of Portugal.
You would be 60 now.

I'm sick of *In Memory,* fluted urns, kabuki-white bikes
on the path to the post office. You promised to haunt me
and you do. Some nights you're a no-show and I am left
with *today-everlasting*, gift baskets of pear and Asiago.

Remember that night at the Surf Club. Since then
I've changed, but my eyes are blue-green still.

Aubade

My ghosts line up, mouths full of bitter
greens and sweet grasses,
names chalked on the walls
of ruined buildings, the night
smelling of their breath.
One wears a split lip,
saxophone-blown. Sometimes he calls
in sick. *I am not your splendid harness.*
Don't wait up. What is sleep anyway.
Barnyard animals, goats and owls sleep.
Even the earth with its seeds and vegetables
rooting underground can rest.
The joists of the house squeak.
Pipes gurgle like stuttering bells
all night. Frost sets a breakfast table.
Butter and milk, clatter of copper.
Watering can from which I wish
to be poured. What can I do
but honor the first silver
hair in the winter comb.

Lovesick Cento

If only I were a root of the tree of the sky.
If only I were the marrow of the alder.
Or else the goodness in the sugarcane of the air.
Whiteness is changing itself into a sugary death.
The broad shouldered block of ivory.
The word Creole all clad in cork.
And the forest when I began to enter it started out
with a tree with cigarette-paper leaves.
The key sings in the door of the unknown room
because of the marvelous blindfolding bandage which
is mine in this blindman's-buff of rending and parting.
It was a good thing you abandoned the wind, the red-
headed waitress, God dying on Friday and revived
on Sunday, fruit of twenty centuries
and the odor of orange trees.
Your bed stretched out across the very sky
in the wine skins of full-blown sheets
which must today be pure azure like a flag,
the door bursting open and shedding oceans.
Let's set fire to the city, so the carousel mermaids
burn, the color of their cheeks become still brighter.
Flames parading in a proud pavane
among roses. The concierge will be looking the other way,
reminded of an entire forest of evergreens in a keyhole.
I summon to me bed linen drying on fences around farms,
that is to say saffron color of tree-rings and of lilacs,
the bestial growl of a raspberry, a dropped hairpin,
nights swallowed in haste. Doorways of your body—
there are nine—and once I opened them all.

Little Black Dress

Puddled at my feet or ruched
to the waist, how easily I shimmied
in and out of you, flicked cigarette ash,
tiny embers, from your bodice, spilled
drinks like rain. You lent style, seriousness.
Unzipped in vans, nests of quilts,
Persian carpets (rug burns on my back),
balled up skin of a selkie. Wingless, plucked,
plumed, aroma of fig pudding, squid ink.
Moths have made a feast of you.
Where is the night we slept on the beach
the morning after, cloud-crusted, glittered
with sand. Give me back the barefoot
sky, tin bucket clattered with shells.

When he said *Sell a book,* I heard *Sail*

I wanted to build a boat and launch for Amsterdam.
Foxtrot on the upper deck in a moon-spangled frock.
I wanted to hold the sky like a bowl, smudge the clouds.
Bring a sentence to its knees. I moved to a spit of land on the coast.
Lit a hurricane lamp in the window. Lined my eyes with kohl.
Wore Goodwill dresses with sun faded sleeves and glass buttons.
My journal entries resembled waves.
I hunted down ink recipes. One called for hawthorn branches cut
in spring and left to dry, the bark pounded, mixed with wine
and iron salt. I pedaled my bicycle through the fishing village.
Buying bread in the Portuguese bakery, met a scalloper
and refused to kiss him, beards not to my taste.
One morning, he appeared on my doorstep clean shaven, nick of cream
at his lip, holding an envelope. Into my cupped hands
he poured whiskers, blond like fields.
All winter, I loved the one who'd lathered and drawn a blade
along his face, run his tongue across the envelope's gummed seal.
In spring, he walked out, and I mixed a new ink: lamp-black,
varnish and egg white. I wrote stories on onionskin.
The pages collected around me, a carpet of paper.

Notes

The epigraph is taken from Federico Garcia Lorca's poem "Gacela of the Dark Death," translated by Catherine Brown.

"I Still Had Two Friends, But They Were Trees" is a line from "The Two Trees," a poem by Larry Levis.

"Bigfoot Walks Among Us" is for Todd McKie, painter of the bluest blues.

"Lovesick Cento" contains lines and fragments by the following: Guillaume Apollinaire, Jean (Hans) Arp, Antonin Artaud, André Breton, René Daumal, Robert Desnos, Paul Éluard, Benjamin Péret, Jacques Prévert, Philippe Soupault and Tristan Tzara.

"Lovesick Cento" is in memory of Alex Londres.

Acknowledgments

Many thanks to the editors of the publications in which these poems first appeared, some with different titles and in different forms.

At Length: "Notes Toward an Elegy"

Bennington Review: "Curriculum Vitae," "Conjoined Twins Plead 'Put Us Back Together,' Brothers Unhappy Since They Were Separated Forty-Five Years Ago," "I Still Had Two Friends, But They Were Trees"

Cherry Tree: "How to Get Released from Hospital"

Cloudbank: "Artisanal Moonshine"

Colorado Review: "Lovesick Cento," "3 Odes: 'To Grief,' 'To Creative Nonfiction,' 'To Wildness'"

Four Way Review: "Aubade," "Soul Wears a Crown of Milk Thistle"

Gulf Coast online: "I Dreamed I Was Venus de Milo"

Little Star 7: "A Guide for Caregivers," "Dear Earth," "Dead Letter Office"

Little Star Weekly: "Bag Boy Works Harder Now That He's a Ghost"

The Massachusetts Review: "When he said *Sell a Book*, I heard *Sail*," "In the Library at the End of the World"

The Missouri Review Poem of the Week: "For an Abandoned Library in Detroit"

The New Republic: "How to Make Dandelion Wine"

Nimrod International Journal: "Plum Jam"

North American Review online: "Black Hole"

On the Seawall: "Doxology," "Great-Great Grandfather Thacker Talks in My Ear"

Pleiades: "Bigfoot Walks Among Us"

Plume: "Braid Him Into the Earth," "Julia," "Little Black Dress"

Southern Humanities Review: "God Awful," "God Denies Any Knowledge of Dead Angel in His Bed"

SWWIM Every Day: "All the Flowers Are for Me"

storySouth: "Insomnia"

Poetry International 27/28: from *The Empress of Serifs*, winner of the 2019 *Poetry International* Winter Chapbook Competition: "A Guide for Caregivers," "Curriculum Vitae" "Dead Letter Office," "Dear Earth," "For an Abandoned Library in Detroit," "Paperwork," "Plum Jam"

Sincere thanks to Philip Hoy and everyone at Waywiser Press for bringing this book into the world. I am indebted particularly to Dora Malech for the insight and close attention she brought to these poems. I'd like to express my deepest gratitude to Paul Muldoon for selecting this manuscript for the Anthony Hecht Poetry Prize and for his generous and invaluable guidance.

My work with Joan Houlihan and Rebecca Morgan Frank at critical junctures helped shape this collection. Thank you as well to friends and colleagues for encouragement and sage advice: Katy Aisenberg, Eric Braude, Elaine Cohen, Vanita Datta, Jenny Grassl, Susan Hankla, Stephen Haven, Kasandra Larsen, Frannie Lindsay, Todd McKie, Lezli Rubin-Kunda, Aimée Sands, Jeffrey Stewart, Joan Wagman and Anna Warrock. Merci to Chris Yeager for spring and all.

Love, abiding, to my teachers, Michael S. Harper and John Hawkes.

Thank you to the Fine Arts Work Center in Provincetown for making my writing life possible. For sustaining support, colossal thanks to the Radcliffe Institute, the Corporation of Yaddo, the National Endowment for the Arts, the Virginia Center for the Creative Arts, and, finally, to The Mount and Straw Dog Writers Guild for an Edith Wharton Writing Residency — complete with fainting couch — which brought me luck.

A Note About the Author

Photo courtesy of Adrianne Mathiowetz

The granddaughter of a Harlan County coal miner, Julia Thacker was raised in Dayton Ohio. She first came to Massachusetts as a fellow at the Fine Arts Work Center in Provincetown. She has also been the recipient of fellowships from the Radcliffe Institute, the Corporation of Yaddo and the National Endowment for the Arts. Her poems appear in *Bennington Review*, *Gulf Coast*, *The Massachusetts Review*, *The New Republic* and *Pleiades*. A portfolio of her work is included in the 25th anniversary issue of *Poetry International*. Julia has taught writing at Tufts University, Radcliffe Seminars and as poet-in-residence in public schools throughout the state. In 2024, she was an Edith Wharton Writer-in-Residence at The Mount. She lives outside of Boston.

A Note About the Anthony Hecht Poetry Prize

The Anthony Hecht Poetry Prize was inaugurated in 2005 and is awarded on an annual basis to the best first or second collection of poems submitted.

FIRST ANNUAL HECHT PRIZE
Judge: J. D. McClatchy
Winner: Morri Creech, *Field Knowledge*

SECOND ANNUAL HECHT PRIZE
Judge: Mary Jo Salter
Winner: Erica Dawson, *Big-Eyed Afraid*

THIRD ANNUAL HECHT PRIZE
Judge: Richard Wilbur
Winner: Rose Kelleher, *Bundle o' Tinder*

FOURTH ANNUAL HECHT PRIZE
Judge: Alan Shapiro
Winner: Carrie Jerrell, *After the Revival*

FIFTH ANNUAL HECHT PRIZE
Judge: Rosanna Warren
Winner: Matthew Ladd, *The Book of Emblems*

SIXTH ANNUAL HECHT PRIZE
Judge: James Fenton
Winner: Mark Kraushaar, *The Uncertainty Principle*

SEVENTH ANNUAL HECHT PRIZE
Judge: Mark Strand
Winner: Chris Andrews, *Lime Green Chair*

EIGHTH ANNUAL HECHT PRIZE
Judge: Charles Simic
Winner: Shelley Puhak, *Guinevere in Baltimore*

NINTH ANNUAL HECHT PRIZE
Judge: Heather McHugh
Winner: Geoffrey Brock, *Voices Bright Flags*

TENTH ANNUAL HECHT PRIZE
Judge: Anthony Thwaite
Winner: Jaimee Hills, *How to Avoid Speaking*

A Note About the Anthony Hecht Poetry Prize

ELEVENTH ANNUAL HECHT PRIZE
Judge: Eavan Boland
Winner: Austin Allen, *Pleasures of the Game*

TWELFTH ANNUAL HECHT PRIZE
Judge: Gjertrud Schnackenberg
Winner: Mike White, *Addendum to a Miracle*

THIRTEENTH ANNUAL HECHT PRIZE
Judge: Andrew Motion
Winner: Christopher Cessac, *The Youngest Ocean*

FOURTEENTH ANNUAL HECHT PRIZE
Judge: Charles Wright
Winner: Katherine Hollander, *My German Dictionary*

FIFTEENTH ANNUAL HECHT PRIZE
Judge: Edward Hirsch
Winner: James Davis, *Club Q*

SIXTEENTH ANNUAL HECHT PRIZE
Judge: Vijay Seshadri
Winner: Danielle Blau, *peep*

SEVENTEENTH ANNUAL HECHT PRIZE
Judge: Alice Fulton
Winner: James D'Agostino, *The Goldfinch Caution Tapes*

EIGHTEENTH ANNUAL HECHT PRIZE
Judge: Linda Gregerson
Winner: Hannah Louise Poston, *Julia Hungry*

NINETEENTH ANNUAL HECHT PRIZE
Judge: Paul Muldoon
Winner: Julia Thacker, *To Wildness*

Other Books from Waywiser

Other Books from Waywiser

Christopher Ricks, ed., *Joining Music with Reason:*
34 Poets, British and American, Oxford 2004-2009
Daniel Rifenburgh, *Advent*
Mary Jo Salter, *It's Hard to Say: Selected Poems*
Alan Shapiro, *By and By*
W. D. Snodgrass, *Not for Specialists: New & Selected Poems*
Mark Strand, *Almost Invisible*
Mark Strand, *Blizzard of One*
Bradford Gray Telford, *Perfect Hurt*
Matthew Thorburn, *This Time Tomorrow*
Cody Walker, *Shuffle and Breakdown*
Cody Walker, *The Self-Styled No-Child*
Cody Walker, *The Trumpiad*
Henry Walters, *The Nature Thief*
Deborah Warren, *The Size of Happiness*
Clive Watkins, *Already the Flames*
Clive Watkins, *Jigsaw*
Richard Wilbur, *Anterooms*
Richard Wilbur, *Mayflies*
Richard Wilbur, *Collected Poems 1943-2004*
Norman Williams, *One Unblinking Eye*
Greg Williamson, *A Most Marvelous Piece of Luck*
Greg Williamson, *The Hole Story of Kirby the Sneak and Arlo the True*
Stephen Yenser, *Stone Fruit*

FICTION
Gregory Heath, *The Entire Animal*
Mary Elizabeth Pope, *Divining Venus*
K. M. Ross, *The Blinding Walk*
Gabriel Roth, *The Unknowns**
Matthew Yorke, *Chancing It*

ILLUSTRATED
Nicholas Garland, *I wish ...*
Eric McHenry and Nicholas Garland, *Mommy Daddy Evan Sage*
Greg Williamson, *The Hole Story of Kirby the Sneak and Arlo the True*

NON-FICTION
Neil Berry, *Articles of Faith: The Story of British Intellectual Journalism*
Irving Feldman, *Usable Truths: Aphorisms & Observations*
Mark Ford, *A Driftwood Altar: Essays and Reviews*
Philip Hoy, *M. Degas Steps Out*
Philip Hoy, ed., *A Bountiful Harvest: The Correspondence of Anthony Hecht and William L. MacDonald*
John Rosenthal, *Searching for Amylu Danzer*
Richard Wollheim, *Germs: A Memoir of Childhood*

*Co-published with Picador